MW00427257

RAFA WRIGHT

To: Malaike

Stay great

wanna know how to achieve financial freedom?

WEALTH

To: Malaikir

WEALTH

Rafa Wright
@fairo_rafa

Plug'd Media 2017
Published in 2017 in Detroit, Michigan
ISBN-13: 978-0996094399
ISBN-10: 0996094393

Thank You:

Jay-Z

Nipsey Hu$$le

E-40

Jay Morrison

Dr. Boyce Watkins

The Honorable Minister Louis Farrakhan

The Honorable Elijah Muhammad

Marcus Garvey

El Hajj Malik El-Shabazz – Malcolm X

M.C. Poole Jr.

Joe Robinson – APX

Royal Lynda Wright

Black folks have been sold a lie about what wealth is. We've been convinced that wealth is material. We get money and spend it foolishly on things that are valueless. Not to say that living life is a bad thing but it is detrimental to invest so much into materialism as we do without plans for retirement, life insurance, or any types of investments. Our culture calls for us to shine but survival also calls for us to be wealthy.

Current statistics on wealth in America state that *the average African American family has a net worth of $17,600* which can be argued down to only $1,700 once you take away depreciated assets which most of our net worth weighs heavily like our vehicles. To the contrary, the average white family in America has a net worth of $171,000. More than half of black families in America have a negative net worth. Historically, black people trends of wealth are increasing but at a dismal rate.

In this book, I look to provide game to my people on wealth building. My goals are simple: To build this generation of African Americans into a wealthier generation. With us being wealthier, our people will be healthier, better educated, better represented, and better civilized. Simply put, people move different when they have money. The reason we get money and remain ignorant because we are still around ignorance. I believe removing the ignorance comes when more of us are wealthier. When all of us have money, the games stop.

A wealthier future can be ours if we seize the opportunities in front of us. We're masters at making sure we're fly. Now, it is time to master getting money, investing, and achieving financial freedom. It is time for us to become wealthy.

This book is subjective as it's my interpretation of what wealth is and how to build individual wealth. However, this book is objective as my opinions have been shaped by testimony, observation, and experiences that have been thoroughly tested and proven. Furthermore, much research has been done on this subject and those studies helped shaped this book.

Before I finish, I want to thank everyone who influenced me to write this work. There's too many people to name but two people I need to address: *Jay-Z* for him forever being a leader of what growth, progression, and wealth is for a person like me. Being black and from the hood, I know anything is possible for what you have done. Most importantly, thank you for releasing *4:44* which is the unofficial soundtrack of this book. Every word in this book is directly influenced by your powerful album of redemption, salvation, black wealth, and overall black excellence.

Lastly, I want to thank Royal Lynda Wright, my daughter who has blessed me with her presence at such a difficult time in the world. Seeing your face every day gives me hope, motivation, and energy to continue to do all that I do. In many ways I think about how risky this type of life is being a person who is unapologetically black and openly working with our people in mind. Not many who take on this task live long or live long comfortably. But if I don't take this ultimate risk, you may not have a fair future. If I don't do this, the struggle continues for your generation. Everything that I am doing, it is for you.

Table of Contents

Section 1.

1. Lack of Generational Wealth
                          - 15
2. Class & Race   - 18
3. Lower Incomes   - 19
4. Student Loans   - 20

Section 2.

5. What is Wealth?   - 23
6. What is Money?   - 25
7. Poor Minded People vs. Wealthy
   Minded People   - 25
8. Being Wealthy vs. Being Poor
                          - 26

9. Understanding Financial Priorities
- 27

Section 3.

10. The Most Important Wealth Rule
- 30

11. Determine Your Net Worth
- 30

12. Components of Net Worth
- 32

13. Budgeting   - 46

14. What liabilities should you be paying
right now?   - 52

15. How to Live?   - 53

16. Living Life?   - 53

17. When should you pay your bills?
- 54

18. Your First Bag   - 57

19. How to view Risk to overcome fear?

                                   - 61

20. Assets for Non-Entrepreneurs

                                   - 62

21. Legitimizing   - 65

Section 4.

22. First Bag Secured   - 71

23. When to Boss Up?   - 71

24. New Budget   - 72

25. How liabilities affect your net worth

                                   - 75

26. Staying within your means

                                   - 76

27. Expanding from your first asset

                                   - 76

28. Diversifying   - 78

29. Securing a Bigger Bag - 80

30. Assets to pursue   - 81

31. Real Estate   - 81

32. Stocks   - 84

33. Bonds   - 89

34. Collectibles   - 90

35. Private Equity   - 91

36. Serial Entrepreneurship

                           - 93

37. Allocating your portfolio

                           - 94

38. Networking   - 96

39. Building a Team   - 96

40. Hiring Help   - 97

41. Credit   - 101

42. Partnerships   - 103

Section 5.

43. The Flip Strategy   - 107

44. The Buy & Hold Strategy

                                - 109

45. The Credit Strategy   - 112

46. Using Multiple Methods - 113

Section 1. Special Circumstances

In the way of you building wealth are special circumstances. I've compiled a list of special circumstances that I believe fits the average person within the culture.

<u>Chapter 1. Lack of Generational Wealth</u>

Perhaps the most pivotal determinant in wealth building is having the advantage of inheriting wealth from a previous generation. An inheritance is not the sole solution for wealth because without an ongoing system in place for the descendant to follow, whatever wealth they inherit will be lost. Nonetheless, being a recipient of generational wealth gives you the head start. *In our culture, the average person only inherits poverty, making wealth building more difficult from a person's time of birth*.

However, lacking generational wealth does not making building wealth impossible, only more difficult. If you really want to be wealthy, stay driven, strive for education on finances, plan, and execute. Furthermore, the best remedy in this special circumstance is to not repeat history for future generations. *In our culture, a repeat lack of wealth is result of many factors, mainly a lack of effort from previous generations and uniquely premature death of previous generation members*. In the unique cases of premature death, life insurance is the remedy. To hedge premature deaths within the culture which are mainly due to poor health and violence, the culture must strive to live healthier, happier lives.

Chapter 2. Class & Race

Wealth and the ability to build wealth has been directly influenced by class and race. In all, wealthier people has the resources to build more wealth and can build wealth easier than poorer people. *Class has been directly influenced by race, with white people having the supreme advantage over everyone else, mostly people of color*. Therefore, some people of color and poorer classed people has had a difficult time building wealth in America. However, building wealth for poorer people of color is not impossible.

Chapter 3. Lower Incomes

Your earning potential while building wealth is of importance, not assuming the more you make, the wealthier you'll be, but in the less you make the more difficult it would be to invest given you have expenses and liabilities that you cannot afford to pay with your current rate of pay. *In our culture, the average person is usually paid less which is directly influenced by class and race*. Therefore, wealth building

will be more difficult for someone
getting paid a wage or salary that
doesn't satisfy their living needs.
However, building wealth is not
impossible.

Chapter 4. Student Loans

Particularly in this generation, student
loan debt will prove to be a problem
with anyone attempting to build wealth.
Many of us have mortgage number
debt amounts in student loans before
we are old enough to think about
buying a home. ***The average***
graduating college student owes an

average of close to $40,000 in student loans. Adding the previous factors, wealth building will be difficult, but again not impossible.

In all, there are many longstanding factors that has held people back in our culture. However, with all the special circumstances in front of us, today has provided plenty of opportunities that we must take advantage of.

Section 2.
What is Wealth?

Chapter 5. What is Wealth?

Wealth is *financial freedom* or the ability to live comfortably for the entirety of your life without financial needs. Wealth is not having lots of money or living lavish because you can live low-key and still be wealthy. Wealthy people are usually rich but rich people aren't necessarily wealthy because a rich person who owes more than he owns isn't wealthy.

Example: An athlete makes $2 million a year after taxes. However, this athlete owes $5 million a year in short term and long-term liabilities. Therefore, instead of being $2 *million rich, this athlete is $3 million poor (**$5 million in debt - $2 million in cash**)*

In all, wealth is a financial system that enables money to work for the person instead of the person working for money. If this system this paying the person a higher income than his expenses, then this person is wealthy. Period!

Poor people can become wealthy just as wealthy people can become poor. The results of whether you're wealthy or poor is your mindset and actions.

Chapter 6. What is Money?

Money is a tool that wealthy people use to make more money while poor people use money as a tool to buy meaningless material items. Poor people work for money while wealthy people make money work for them.

Chapter 7. Poor Minded People vs. Wealthy Minded People

Poor minded people use money foolishly while wealthy minded people use money wisely. There are people within the culture that's cash rich but poor minded which translates in their financial behavior. In all, these people won't be rich for long and will never be wealthy.

By contrast, there are people within the culture that is cash poor but wealthy minded and its translated in their financial behavior. In all, these types of people won't be poor for long and will eventually be very wealthy.

Chapter 8. Being Wealthy vs. Being Poor

Most of all, wealthy people are in control of their lives because of their financial freedom. Wealthy people can move as they wish. By contrast, poor people are controlled their entire lives because their financial freedom is in the hands of someone else. Poor people are told when and how to move because they don't have financial freedom.

Chapter 9. Understanding Financial Priorities

Perhaps the most pivotal step in pursuing wealth is understanding what financial priorities are in your life. Understanding what is important when it comes to your finances and making the right choices when you make money is just as important as making money itself. Living life is fine when planned and budgeted for, especially after you planned for a wealthy future. Most of all, to be wealthy you must prioritize investing more than you do flexing.

Sometimes it's cool to floss but don't buy an $85,000 car before you buy a house
– E-40

Section 3: Come-Up

Chapter 10. The Most Important Wealth Rule

The one rule to remember when pursuing wealth is that *wealth doesn't come overnight so you must be patient, disciplined, and persistent.*

Chapter 11. Determine your Net Worth

Men lie, women lie. Numbers don't.

- Jay Z

Your *net worth* is where your pockets are at this very moment. You can determine your net worth by *subtracting all your liabilities from your assets.*

Net Worth = Assets – Liabilities

The higher your net worth, the wealthier you are. The lower your net worth, the more broke you are. If you have a negative net worth, then you are worth nothing.

The average African American family has a net worth of $1,400.

The average white American family has a net worth of $171,000.

Chapter 12. Components of Net Worth

An *asset* is something of value that makes you money and wealthy. Assets either generate money or *appreciation* which is a rise in value.

> I bought some artwork for $1 million. 2 years later, that shit worth $2 million. Few years later, that worth $8 million. I can't wait to give this shit to my children.
>
> - Jay Z

Most of all, an asset is money working for you instead of you working for money.

Assets

Risk is the danger associated with an asset and is the determinant that makes an asset valuable. The riskier the asset, the higher the reward. The lower the risk, the lower the reward.

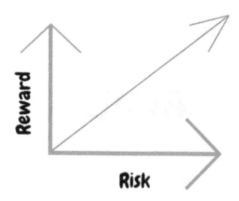

Theoretically, *the younger you are, the more risks you should take*.

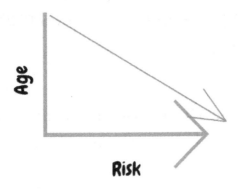

Risks differ per asset and per person.
It is up you to determine what risks are
ideal for you.

Take a risk! You gotta shoot to miss!
- Fabolous

Risk also brings about the possibility of
loss. The possibility of losing
everything is unavoidable when

pursuing wealth but chances makes champions.

Can't be a boss if you never took a loss!
- Rocko

A *liability* is an expense or something that makes you less wealthy.

There are two types of liabilities: *Avoidable liabilities* are expenses that don't have to be in your life. *Unavoidable liabilities* are expenses that you cannot avoid. Sometimes a liability may fall under both categories.

Example: you need food to survive (unavoidable). However, what you eat is the difference between an unavoidable liability and an avoidable liability. If you can't afford to eat steak and lobster, you shouldn't be buying steak and lobster (avoidable). If you can only afford salad, then eat salad.

Of these two types of liabilities, they are either **short term** which are expenses due month to month (or within a year) or **long term** which are expenses due past a year.

You got to learn the difference between guns and butter. There are two types of niggas, niggas with guns, and niggas with butter. What are the guns? That's the real estate, the stocks and bonds, art work. Shit that appreciates with value. What's the butter? Cars, clothes, jewelry, all the bullshit that don't mean shit after you buy it. That's what it's all about: Guns and butter baby! You lil dumb motherfuckas!"

- Ving Rhames

You can determine your net worth by creating a **balance sheet** which outlines all your assets and liabilities. **NOTE**: what's below isn't a formal balance sheet. However, it's an easy format to measure your pockets.

(1) take a sheet of paper,

(2) draw a line up the middle,

(3) on the left side which is titled "assets," list everything that puts money in your pocket,

(4) on the right side which is titled "liabilities," list everything that takes money out of your pocket,

(5) subtract the right from the left.

Balance Sheet

Assets	Liabilities
Salary = 36,000	Student Loans = 50,000
	Rent = 7,250
	Car Note = 3,600
	Food = 5,000
	Cable/Internet = 1,500
	TV = 120
	TIDAL = 160
	Apple Music = 120
	Clothes = 10,000
	Shoes = 8,000
	Vacation = 2,000
	Club = 1,800
	Gas Money = 1,200
	unpaid tickets = 1,800
	driver's license reinstate = 250
	Childcare = 3,000
	Warrants = 3,550
= 36,000	= 99,250

-63,250

40

The difference between your liabilities and assets is your net worth.

Common assets of wealthy people are:

- *Businesses* - Entrepreneurial ventures.
- *Real estate* - Land and property.
- *Stocks* - Shares of ownership in private and public enterprises.
- *Bonds* - IOUs to companies and governments.
- *Collectibles* - Rare, coveted, valuable items.

There are two types of assets: **Active assets** which require your hands-on work. **Passive assets** are assets which do not require your hands-on work. Sometimes an active asset can become a passive asset and a passive asset can become an active asset.

Example: Your first asset, a small business you started 10 years ago is doing great. You work as the general manager, making this business an active asset. However, you think the business can survive without you, so you hire a replacement for your position which relieves your duty, making this business a passive asset.

Example1: Your car wash business has been a passive asset for the past 3 years since you retired from managing the business. However, your new manager has left the business worst off than it was before you retired. So, you decide to come out of retirement to work as the manager of the car wash, making it an active asset.

In assets, there are 3 classes of risk:

- **Low Risk** - presents the lowest return.
- **Medium Risk** - presents a moderate return.
- **High Risk** - presents the highest return.

Common liabilities from our culture
are:

- *Expensive clothes*
- *Expensive cars*
- *Jewelry*
- *Extracurricular activities*
- *Drug habits*
- *Unplanned children*
- *Some relationships*

Basically, a lifestyle that you can't
afford is usually the most common
liability most of us take on.

In all, wealth is truly measured when
one has more assets than liabilities.

Assets > Liabilities

Your disposable income is what you'll use to start building wealth.
Disposable income is the money that's left over once you get paid and pay all expenses. This is the money you will use to invest.

Disposable Income = Income - Liabilities/Expenses

Income comes in two forms: *Active income* is income you directly worked for. *Passive income* is income generated from money working for you without your direct work.

Chapter 13. Budgeting

You must create a budget. Your budgeting objectives are to:

- **Start a rainy-day fund**
- **Start investing**
- **Reduce liabilities**

A **rainy-day fund** is for emergencies. You should aim to stack 4-6 months of your monthly expenses.

Example: Your monthly expenses total $1500. Therefore, you should aim to have $6000 - $9000 stacked up in case something happens to you financially.

Rainy Day Fund = Your monthly expenses X 4-6 months

The easiest way to create a rainy-day fund is to **pay yourself the moment you get paid**. There's no set amount on how much to pay yourself because everyone doesn't make the same but **pay yourself at least 10% of your pay every time you get paid**.

Example: If you make $1500 a month, you should save at least $150 a month for a rainy day.

Even though you set a savings goal of 10% or whatever you choose, you should be working to lower your expenses. But as you lower expenses, you should remain the same savings, even increasing your savings.

Example: Continuing from the previous example, If you reduce your expenses from $1500 to $1200, your savings should remain $1500 or even increase with your newly freed money.

Next you need **bag money** which is the money you will start investing with. Again, there's no specific amount you need to start investing but *I would apply at least 30% of your pay towards investing*.

Example: Continuing from the previous example, you should put away $450 of your monthly income to start investing.

If the asset you're pursuing cost more than one month's worth of savings, save for multiple months until you have enough.

Example: Continuing from the previous 2 examples, your first asset costs $1000 but you can only save $450 a month so you save for three months then you invest.

An alternative to saving the bag money is applying both your rainy-day money and bag money together to make an investment.

Example: Continuing from the previous 3 examples, instead of saving $450 a month towards your first asset, you're saving $600 a month towards your first asset ($150 rainy day money + $450 bag money). Instead of waiting 3 months, you can buy your first asset in 2 months.

A reason you would want to invest your emergency money is because **cash is the worst investment to have**. Money just sitting won't generate any wealth, so you must keep your money invested. Yes, you risk losing your savings due to risk but at this point what do you have to lose? After you've paid yourself and invested, the rest will go towards expenses.

Example: Continuing from the previous 4 examples, your remaining funds total $900.

Chapter 14. What liabilities should you be paying right now?

Only pay your current, priority expenses at this point (rent, food, utilities, transportation, medical, childcare). Your goal must be to lower your expenses as low as possible. You must postpone long term expenses and avoidable liabilities at this time altogether. You'll have to eliminate everything that's extra from your expenses (partying, clothes, shoes, belts, excessive lifestyle).

Chapter 15. How to live?

You must *live below your means*.
Shop for deals, buy items on sale, buy
in bulk, buy used, and always plan
your spending. Never shop on impulse
and always look for a bargain.

Chapter 16. Living Life

Right now, you shouldn't be thinking
about enjoying yourself or anything
pleasurable. Fun is your best
distraction and should be avoided at
this time.

Chapter 17. When should you pay your bills?

You should pay your bills on the last day of your **grace period** which is the time that's allowed to customers after the bill's official due date.

Example: Your car note is due on the 3rd of every month. However, you have a grace of 3 extra days which allows you to pay your bills on the 6th of every month.

You should pay your bills on its grace period deadline to give you more time to maximize an asset you've invested in.

Example: If your bills are due on the 1st of the month with 7-day grace periods and you have an asset that turns profit every 5 days, you can invest the money you would've paid your bills with and generate an extra profit.

Socially, you should be out the way right now, away from any distractions that will pull money away from your wealth goals. Some activities will have to be lessened or eliminated altogether. Some people you may have to distance yourself from temporarily or permanently. Your focus is in the balance if you don't fall back.

Pay yourself first, invest and starve out your liabilities

For help with budgeting, check out books and videos by *@therealboycewatkins* and budgeting sites like *Mint*.

Dr. Boyce Watkins -
@therealboycewatkins
www.boycewatkins.com

Mint
www.mint.com

<u>Chapter 18. Your First Bag</u>

Your first asset should be an entrepreneurial venture. Your best odds would be becoming an entrepreneur yourself, even if part time.

Aside from investing money, you will have to actively manage this business to make sure it generates money successfully. Apart of your management will be to figure out your break even points and when to reinvest, or *reup*.

Example: An online clothing store owner invested $500 into her business. With all costs added, her pieces are $7 per unit. She will sell her pieces for $20 per unit (71 units total). Once she has sold 25 units, she will hit her break-even point.

The speed at which your asset is producing will be your indicator to boss up or play it steady.

Example: Continuing from the previous example, the online store owner sold 25 units within 3 days which gives her the indication that business is going great and that she needs to reup and expand her line.

When your investment needs to expand, use your profits as reinvestment funds.

Example: A clothing designer starts a clothing line with $500. This business generates $1500 in revenue, netting the clothing designer $1000 in profit. The clothing designer then reinvests his initial investment of $500 plus $500 from his profits, increasing the total investment to $1000.

Continuing to reinvest more and more money into your assets will keep your money working for you. Also, constantly reinvesting keeps your money tied up so you don't have the luxury to spend it on useless things. Another thing, make sure the assets you invest in are in style.

Example: In the current digital climate, newspapers and print magazines have suffered in sales. Therefore, one could argue these newspaper companies are out of style.

You don't want to invest in a bad asset that won't make money so planning your moves is the most key of all processes.

Aside from investing in the assets that's going to secure your first bag, other assets you are going to need is *insurance for your life and health*.

Any asset that you don't understand or know how to manage should be avoided. Right now, invest in what you can afford and in what you know how to handle.

Chapter 19. How to view Risk to overcome fear?

The best way to overcome fear in investing is to adopt the **YOLO** attitude towards investing. If the motto "You Only Live Once" can encourage you to live life, then that same motto can help you overcome the fears of losing your money in an investment. ***Instead of saying, "You only live once so ball out" say, "You only live once so get money!"***

Chapter 20. Assets for non-entrepreneurs

If you don't want to hustle, you can still invest and build. Ideal investments for non-entrepreneurs are going to more than likely generate a passive income or appreciation from the start and won't require work from the investor.

Ideal assets for the non-entrepreneur are:

- **401(k)**
- **Stocks**
- **Bonds**
- **Index mutual funds**

Just because you're not entrepreneurial doesn't mean that you cannot build wealth. In all, **wealth building isn't about speed as much as its about participation and consistency.** Ideally, wealth isn't built overnight but rather over the working life of the average person. Yes, you may become wealthy faster as an entrepreneur, but you may become wealthy faster as an employee, so your work status shouldn't be the determinant to whether you pursue wealth or not. In all, wealth is achievable regardless to whether you work for yourself or someone else.

<u>Chapter 21. Legitimizing</u>

You need to make sure your pursuit of wealth is legal. You'll do that by:

- **Forming a LLC**
- **Paying your taxes**

In most cases, by forming a limited liability company (LLC) you are protecting your assets from personal liability.

Example: You form a LLC to buy real estate. You have personal debts totaling $50,000. By forming a LLC, whoever you owe $50,000 to will have no legal right to the real estate holdings you have in your LLC.

Being that most of us have debt in some form, you must work to protect whatever assets you may have while you're getting your money right. You can't protect your assets from all debt (the government can seize your assets regardless) so you have to prioritize to eventually pay off all of your debts, but in the meantime, forgo what you can and have a repayment plan for the unavoidable debts.

By paying taxes, you pay the price of building wealth in America. The government will leave you be to continue wealth when you pay taxes. Furthermore, the government will provide breaks and opportunities for you to make more money just because your wealthy.

Summary

It only takes a mental transformation, planning, a small financial investment, consistency, and patience to start building wealth. Think about what so many others from our culture would do with just $500: invest in things worth nothing.

From this perspective, you see the opportunity costs you have that either makes you wealthy or broke. It's up to you to make the right choice.

Your pursuit of wealth starts with you assessing your current financial situation, budgeting, and making your initial investment. Most of all, your wealth chase is fueled by your hunger for more. You are making all kinds of adjustments to get this first bag. Once this first bag is secured, it'll be used to secure more bags. Soon you'll be wealthy, but you must stay focused.

Section 4:
Bossing Up

Chapter 22. First Bag Secured

Once you've secured your first bag, those funds will be used to secure other bags.

Multiple incomes are the keys to building wealth.

Chapter 23. When to Boss Up?

Only when you've secured your first bag is when you should chase another bag. Don't bite off more than you can chew or move before you should.

Example: You open a barber shop that's going great but still hasn't broke even. But,

you're working to open another barber shop
without the first shop being solidified.

Chapter 24. New Budget

Once you start making money from
your investment or investments, you
should start budgeting to **eliminate
any long-term liabilities you have,
all while still investing and
controlling your short-term
expenses**. Your elimination plan
should be dependent on your security
and income potential.

Example: You have assets that guarantees you $200,000 a year. You have short term expenses totaling $30,000 a year and long-term expenses totaling $120,000. Over the past 5 years, you've saved $100,000 so you decide to pay off your long-term debt along with paying your short-term expenses for the year.

Example1: You have assets that has averaged $100,000 over the past 5 years, some years producing higher profits than others. You have short term expenses totaling $30,000 a year and long-term expenses totaling $120,000. Although you've saved $50,000, you are less secure because of your everchanging returns on *your assets, so you decide to create a 3-year plan to eliminate a third of your long-term debt every year until it's gone.*

Although you should be paying your long-term debt off sooner than later, you shouldn't be thinking about paying off any long-term debt until you have guaranteed money coming from your assets and money saved for a rainy day.

Chapter 25. How Liabilities affect your Net Worth

In all, the more liabilities you have, the less wealthy you are, regardless of how many assets you have.

Example: A person worth $100,000 with only $10,000 ($90,000 in assets) in liabilities is far more attractive than a person worth $200,000 ($350,000 in assets) with $150,000 in liabilities.

You have more opportunities to invest when you have less of your money owed to liabilities.

Chapter 26. Staying within you means

Regardless of how much money you're making, you must stay within your means, ideally living below your means. In all, understand what your bare minimums are, set a limit on fun, and stick with your program to better position yourself.

Chapter 27. Expanding from your first Asset

Once you've secured your first bag, you can work on a new bag. It will be easier to venture within the same industry that you secured your first bag in.

Example: A successful hairdresser decides to branch off into hair care products. Because she has built a strong client base and a strong following within the hair industry, she has been able to turn her hair care products into a successful venture.

Although possibly more challenging, you can venture into a new industry altogether.

Example: An eBay store owner that sells used clothing under $10 per item has made enough money to start investing into real *estate. Now aside from running a full time eBay store, the owner now has real estate holdings for sale and rent.*

At this point, venturing into a new industry should be easier versus before when you lacked the financial backing to pay for the needed help. Now, you have the funds and resources to turn a success quicker.

Chapter 28. Diversifying

Diversification is having multiple investments. Diversification creates multiple incomes, widens your portfolio and hedges possible losses to your portfolio. When one asset is underperforming, another asset can overperform which offsets the losses from the underperforming asset.

Example: A food truck owner who makes enough money to survive in one season but losses all income in the other three seasons of the year. So, the food truck owner has rental properties and runs an online store to hedge the loss of income from the food truck.

Diversification = Multiple sources of income, hedges losses, widens portfolio.

Chapter 29. Securing a Bigger Bag

Once you've secured your first bag, use that bag to get a bigger bag. Take your proceeds and invest in a larger-producing asset.

Example: After you've started and operated a successful hair salon which nets you $50,000 in profit a year, you save and invest $100,000 into real estate which will net you $90,000 in profit a year.

Your new assets must generate more wealth than your previous assets. ***Don't boss down and hustle backwards***.

Chapter 30. Assets to pursue

Regardless of how you secured your first bag, your bigger bags should be in proven assets that will protect your money and make you more wealth, such as:

- *Real Estate*
- *Stocks*
- *Bonds*
- *Private Equity*
- *Serial Entrepreneurship*

Chapter 31. Real Estate

Real Estate is land ownership. *Those who own the land controls the economy*. Residentially, everyone on earth needs shelter. Commercially, there will always be a need for storefronts, offices, and storage space.

Real estate can generate an income and an appreciation of **equity** which is your ownership in the property. So, you are increasing your net worth in two ways: cash and worth.

Example: You purchased a rental property for $10,000. Once you find a tenant, this asset will generate $800 a month in rent. Also, you get your property appraised and the value of the property is $30,000 which $20,000 more than what you paid. With the *rent revenues and the appreciation of equity, your investment is paying you in two ways.*

Ideally, start with residential real estate because it's a cheaper entry cost, lower barrier of entry, and a wide variety of spaces. Once you've gotten a hang of residential properties, you can graduate to commercial properties. For more in-depth knowledge on real estate, check out the movement of ***@mrjaymorrison***. Jay Morrison is a real estate investor with holdings all over America. Morrison teaches real estate to citizens from the hood through his Jay Morrison Academy and even has a crowd-investment company for real estate named the Tulsa Real Estate Fund that allows people to invest small amounts of money into large real estate development projects.

Jay Morrison - @mrjaymorrison
www.jaymrrealestate.com
www.tulsarealestatefund.com

Entry Cost: $1,000 - $10,000

Chapter 32. Stocks

Stock is a share of ownership in a company. When you buy a share of stock, you are buying the right to a company's profits and losses. You buy stock from stock exchanges like *the New York Stock Exchange (NYSE), or the Over-The-Counter-Bulletin-Board (OTCBB) for penny stocks*. These exchanges use brokerage firms like *Charles Schwab* or discount brokers like *E*TRADE*, or *Robinhood*. Like real estate, your investment in this asset can generate an income through *dividends* which is a portion of the company's profits paid out to stockholders or appreciation with rising stock prices.

Example: You buy 1,000 shares of a company at $15 per share (1,000 shares X $15 = $15,000). This company pays a quarterly dividend of $1 per share ($1 per share X 1,000 shares = $1,000 X 4 quarters = $4,000 a year). Also, the stock price increased from $15 per share to $20 per share making your overall investment worth $20,000.

Ideally, you would want to start with at least $5,000 to maximize dividends and appreciations when they occur. **With stocks, the more you own the more you'll earn**.

Example: You buying 1 share of a company a week will not generate the type of profits that buying 25 shares of a company a week would.

Your best option would be to buy large quantity of stocks because stocks can only be effective when you buy large quantities of stock. One share won't make you wealthy. Hundreds and thousands of shares will make you wealthy. Once you buy them, hold them, allow them to pay you dividends and appreciate, reinvest the dividends to generate even more appreciation, then sell them once they are trading above market price. For more information about investing in stocks, I would recommend visiting *Investopedia* which has a world of information about strategies, concepts, prices, and trends. Also, books to read are ***Buffetology, The Intelligent Investor***, and ***Security Analysis***. These books break down the nature of investing in stocks while exploring my preferred investing strategy called Value Investing.

Entry Cost = $5,000 - UP

Chapter 33. Bonds

Bonds are basically loans from you to banks, companies, and governments. When you buy a bond, they are to be repaid with interest. When you buy a bond, the company will pay you interest over a specified time. Once this time is up, you'll get your principal investment back.

Example: You buy a bond for $10,000 which guaranteed you $500 a year for 10 years ($500 X 10 years = $5,000). After this 10-year period, the company who issued the bond will return your initial investment of $10,000.

Bonds are great, safe assets, especially when other assets are underperforming. Ideally, *you would want to invest in grade AAA corporate or government bonds to ensure your interest*.

Entry Cost = $1,000 - UP

Chapter 34. Collectibles

Collectibles are valuable items that are rare or highly coveted. Collectibles could be artwork, precious metals, sports cards, comics, or other items that are collected for value.

Chapter 35. Private Equity

Private equity is buying ownership in a private small business. Ownership in a company entitles you to that company's profits and losses. Basically, a private equity investment is investing in someone else. These types of investments could produce income and appreciation. In some cases, being an early investor in a private business could make you very rich if that company does very well.

Example: You invest $10,000 into your girlfriend's hair business for 50% ownership. Within a year, this hair business produces

$200,000 in revenue. Your $10,000 investment has been maximized a hundred times over.

You must have your money right because private equity investments are expensive and very risky. You will need some other assets in place working and money stacked for a rainy day. Nonetheless, private equity assets are some of the highest profit producing assets that exist.

Entry Cost = $10,000 - UP

Chapter 36. Serial Entrepreneurship

Perhaps the best thing you can do with your bag is start more businesses. The best returns will be in entrepreneurship.

Example: You start a beauty supply store on the eastside in 2017. In 2018, your store makes $250,000 in profit so you decide to open a store on the westside. Now, you have 2 stores making $250,000 in profit. Then, you open another store and that makes $250,000.

Being entrepreneurial allows you to generate the most wealth while contributing to the economy through job creation and opportunities for wealth building with others.

Entry Cost = $500 - UP

Chapter 37. Allocating your portfolio

Allocation is managing your portfolio's performance to maximize profits and limit losses when you have multiple assets.

Example: In your $250,000 investment portfolio, you have $125,000 invested in your best performing asset, $25,000 in your second best performing asset, and $100,000 in your third best performing asset.

The moment you realize you have an ill asset in your portfolio, you must make an instant reallocation.

Example: Continuing from the previous example, realizing your second best performing asset is underinvested, you decide to lower your holdings in your third best performing asset and increase holdings in your second best performing asset.

To maintain your wealth, you will always be allocating and reallocating your investments.

Chapter 38. Networking

You must build connections and relationships to elevate your wealth. A strong network allows you access to valuable information and resources you'll need to level up even further.

Wealth is about what you do to get it and who you know to keep it.

Chapter 39. Building a Team

To elevate your game, you'll need to build a crew. Your crew should include:

- *Lawyer* - handles the legal issues.

- ***Consultant*** - knows industries or knows the people who knows industries.
- ***Investor*** - has funds and assets to finance projects.
- ***Accountant*** - handles the financial issues.

You should be scouting for your crew when you're networking.

Chapter 40. Hiring Help

Eventually, you will need to hire others to help you maintain and grow. Your workers will:

- ***Lighten your workload***
- ***Bring specialization***

- ***Spread the wealth and opportunity***

Example: You own and operate a grocery store on the south side which has been successful for 10 years. Now, you are ready to open another store on the north-side, so you decide to hire a new, experienced general manager for the south side location and you will take over as the new general manager of the north side location.

The risk of hiring help is hiring the wrong people. The only defense against hiring the wrong people is thorough background checks, checking resumes, and taking references from your network.

The most key reason to hire help is to have a specialist working for you which can take your investments to the next level. Experts in specialized fields know how to work an asset in ways you may not, so having them working for you makes you even wealthier.

Example: You have an investment firm that invests in stocks, private equity, and real estate. You invest $100,000 and generates $100,000 in profit over the next 5 years ($20,000 a year). You are masterful at

general management, but you have no
expert knowledge in real estate or stock
investing. So, you decide to hire an
experienced manager in real estate and an
experienced manager in stock investing.
After these hires, both managers take your
$200,000 investment ($100,000 initial
investment + $100,000 in profit) and turns it
into $750,000 in just 1 year.

Your first hires should work your first
asset because it should be the most
matured and should require less of
you. Also, your first asset shouldn't
require much repair in case things
don't work out with your hires. In fields

you're not as knowledgeable in, you need to hire someone in the beginning. Regardless of what asset you hire help for, this worker needs to be an expert.

Most of all, you hiring others spreads the wealth, creating opportunities for others to create wealth for themselves. More money can be made and distributed which is the goal of wealth.

Chapter 41. Credit

Access to outside money from investors and banks will be easier to get to once you become wealthy.

Using credit could help you secure an even bigger bag but with someone else's money.

Example: You want to purchase a commercial space for $250,000. You've established good credit to get financed by a bank which gives you a long-term loan over 10 years. Over the course of 10 years, this property has made you $4 million. Within 5 years, you repay your loan, your interest, and made money without putting up a dollar.

Credit is an instrument you must use with caution. Nonetheless, it's a great tool for the wealthy to raise funds

and make money without using your
own money.

Chapter 42. Partnerships

***Wealth is best accumulated when
done in groups***. Partnerships spread
the risk but increases the profit. Most
of all, your partners and you all bring
different degrees of expertise and
networks which makes the level up
easier.

<u>Summary</u>

Once you make some money, your goal is to convert it into wealth. Once you build wealth, you must work to grow it and keep it which is much more difficult than accumulating it in the first place. During this time, you must master networking, and building a team of people that'll help you get wealthier, faster. Your mental should be sharper than ever. You should be moving like someone who is worth something instead of moving recklessly. *Most of all, you should be thinking about the big picture: Your safety and security, your family's* *safety and security, and the health* *of your team and community*. In all, once you're given the opportunity to eat, you better make sure you're always in position to eat.

> "If you from the streets though, there's plenty of loopholes to eat yo. Once they let you in, you suppose to keep dough."
>
> - **Jadakiss (Things I been through)**

Section 5: Strategies

Section 5 will cover the basic strategies of wealth building. Remember the order of how money flows for wealthy people: *Invest First, Spend Afterwards.*

Chapter 43. The Flip Strategy

Flipping is buying something and selling it. Flipping creates income and profit. *The wealth is in asset being bought and sold and the cash/profit generated*. The speed which you flip something depends on what's being sold. Some assets will sell faster than others, but some will generate higher profits than others. ***Overall, you must buy your inventories low and sell them high***. The higher you sell, the more you profit. The faster you sell, the quicker you profit.

Example: Homes may take longer to sell than clothing. However, in most cases selling a home will generate a higher profit than clothing.

Ideally in the beginning, you should flip cheap inventories that will sell fast like clockwork. As you get your money up, start buying more expensive assets to flip. These items may take longer to

sell but when they sell you will get
more money.

Chapter 44. The Buy & Hold
Strategy

When you buy and hold an asset, your
intentions are appreciation. You will
buy an asset at one value with the
hopes of the value going up over time.
***You must buy low and hold until the
price is high enough for your needs***.

*Example: You buy $100,000 worth of stock
over a 10-year period for an average of $10
per share. 20 years later after you stopped*

buying stock, the company's stock is worth $90 per share.

You must make sure you are buying and holding an asset that's worth holding. ***The wealth is in the asset being bought and sold, the asset price at purchase, the price's appreciation, and the selling price of the asset***.

Example: You bought clothing which is better off selling fast than holding because of the immediate value in the current style.

Example1: You bought a piece of art for $1 million that's worth $1.8 million. The next week, someone offers you $1.5 million. However, it's been estimated that this piece of art will be worth $10 million in 5 years. Therefore, you are better off holding the asset to maximize the profit potential.

Buying and holding is a practice best for those with other assets working for them. If you are on a come-up, then you may want to wait before utilizing this practice.

Chapter 45. The Credit (Middle Man) Strategy

Another strategy for the well-off wealth builder is using credit to buy assets. You will need an established reputation beforehand to get credit. When using credit, you are usually buying assets that will generate an income or an asset to flip. In most cases, you wouldn't want to buy and hold an asset with credit. *The wealth is in the wealth builder's credit reputation, the asset being bought, and the use of that asset (whether it*

**will be used to generate an income
or sold to generate an income).**

Chapter 46. Using Multiple Strategies

Using multiple methods will maximize diversification, resulting in the greatest increase in wealth.

Example: In December of this year, you create plans to diversify. In January, you invest in a mobile food business. Your inventory, food, is flipped on the truck. By June, you have enough money to buy your first buy and hold asset, stock in Nike. With your first asset still flipping, you're able to buy another buy and hold asset at the end of the year but with credit, a rental property.

Remember to practice allocation.

*Example1: Continuing from the previous example, when monitoring your portfolio, you conclude that your first asset, the mobile food truck, is your best performing asset, your rental property is your second best performing asset, and your stocks are your third best performing asset. In total, your asset is worth $250,000 (**$100,000 from the mobile food truck, $100,000 in stock, and $50,000 in the rental property**).*

After noticing your second best performing asset (rental property) is underinvested, you *sell $50,000 of your stock and invest the proceeds into more real estate. Now, you have $100,000 in your mobile food truck, $100,000 in real estate, and $50,000 in stock.*

Lastly, to eliminate the debt from your first rental property, you take your profits from the rental properties and pay off the debt you picked up to buy it.

Remember to use your team and network to help you theorize every move while diversifying in this matter.

Outro

If there is anything about wealth that I didn't include in the meat of this book and that is how important wealth is with creating an easier life for future generations. **Generational wealth** is key for our children, and their children, and so on. Besides yourself, you should want to build wealth for your future descendants. Besides yourself and them, you should want to build wealth for your community. The greatest advantages of wealthy people are head-starts. **Whites, Arabs, Asians, and other groups that are** *ever-wealthy today is a direct result of generational wealth*. *However, this generational wealth was still built which gives us hope as black people who has nothing to lose*. We can truly build ourselves to the capacity of disrupting and changing the lives for our entire race for centuries to come.

Let's continue to be fly and socially influential. But let's really get money and put it to good use for the culture.

My social enterprise ***Urban Plug L3C*** launched Us Food Market, an upcoming grocery store in Detroit. ***Us Food Market will be the only black-owned full-service grocery store in what's considered America's blackest city***. You can contribute to helping make Us Food Market happening via GoFundMe now –

www.rafawright.com

Thank You!!!!!!

96526972R00068

Made in the USA
Columbia, SC
30 May 2018